From Metal to Bicycle

by Avery Toolen

Bullfrog Books

Ideas for Parents and Teachers

Bullfrog Books let children practice reading informational text at the earliest reading levels. Repetition, familiar words, and photo labels support early readers.

Before Reading

- Discuss the cover photo. What does it tell them?

- Look at the picture glossary together. Read and discuss the words.

Read the Book

- "Walk" through the book and look at the photos. Let the child ask questions. Point out the photo labels.

- Read the book to the child, or have him or her read independently.

After Reading

- Prompt the child to think more. Ask: Do you like to ride bicycles? Have you ever thought about where bicycles come from?

Bullfrog Books are published by Jump!
5357 Penn Avenue South
Minneapolis, MN 55419
www.jumplibrary.com

Library of Congress Cataloging-in-Publication Data

Names: Toolen, Avery, author.
Title: From metal to bicycle / by Avery Toolen.
Description: Minneapolis, MN: Jump! Inc., [2022]
Series: Where does it come from? | Includes index.
Audience: Ages 5–8 | Audience: Grades K–1
Identifiers: LCCN 2020047825 (print)
LCCN 2020047826 (ebook)
ISBN 9781645279761 (hardcover)
ISBN 9781645279778 (paperback)
ISBN 9781645279785 (ebook)
Subjects: LCSH: Bicycles—Juvenile literature.
Metal-work—Juvenile literature.
Classification: LCC TL412 .T66 2022 (print)
LCC TL412 (ebook) | DDC 629.227/2—dc23
LC record available at https://lccn.loc.gov/2020047825
LC ebook record available at https://lccn.loc.gov/2020047826

Editor: Eliza Leahy
Designer: Michelle Sonnek

Photo Credits: Shutterstock, cover; stockphotograf/Shutterstock, 1, 12–13, 22br; adventtr/iStock, 3; Sergey Novikov/Shutterstock, 4, 20–21, 22bl; kaband/Shutterstock, 5, 23tr; OVHNHR/Shutterstock, 6–7, 22tl, 23tl; INDONESIAPIX/Shutterstock, 8–9, 10, 22tr, 23tm, 23bl, 23bm, 23br; Eshma/Shutterstock, 11; Nomad_Soul/Shutterstock, 14; Lim Yong Hian/Shutterstock, 15; ZUMA Press, Inc./Alamy, 16–17; photo-denver/Shutterstock, 18–19, 22bm; Natykach Nataliia/Shutterstock, 24.

Printed in the United States of America at Corporate Graphics in North Mankato, Minnesota.

Table of Contents

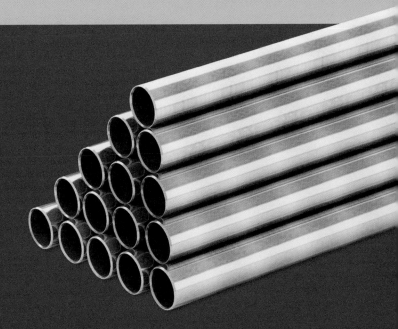

From Metal

Bea rides a bike!

Where does it come from?

Iron!
It is a kind of metal.
It is mined.

iron ore

iron

Iron goes to a factory.

It is heated.

Then it cools.

Now it is steel!
It is cut into tubes.

steel
tubes

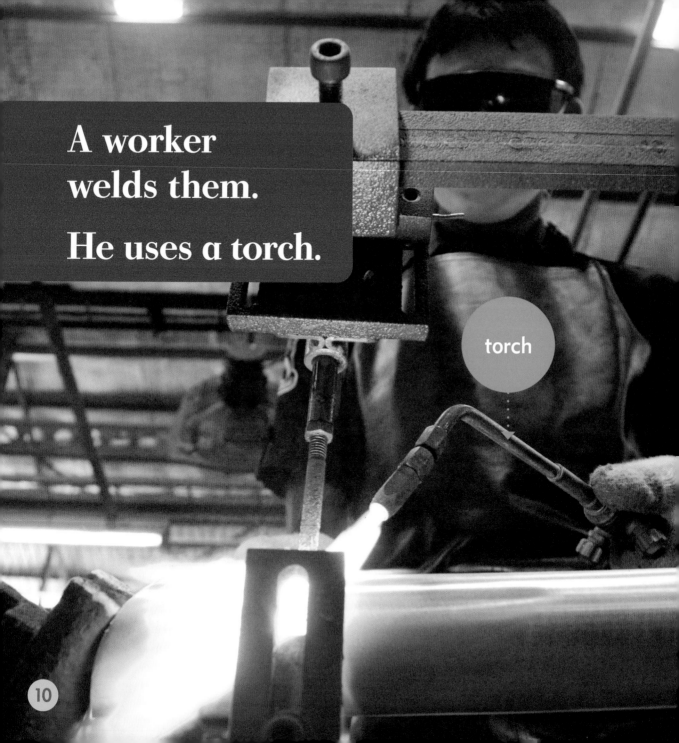

A worker
welds them.

He uses a torch.

torch

frame

He makes a frame!

paint
sprayer

12

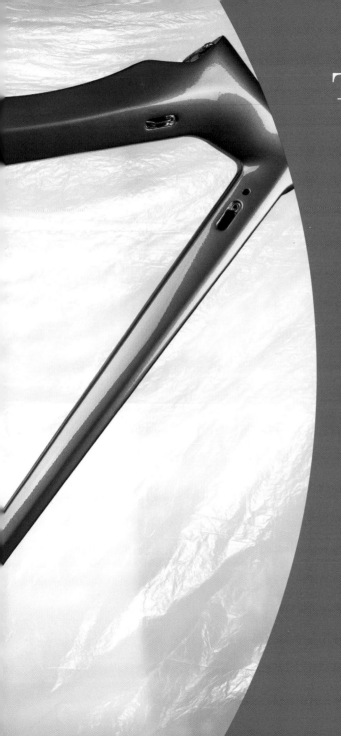

Then he paints it.
He uses a
paint sprayer.
Cool!

A spoke tool helps build wheels.

spoke tool

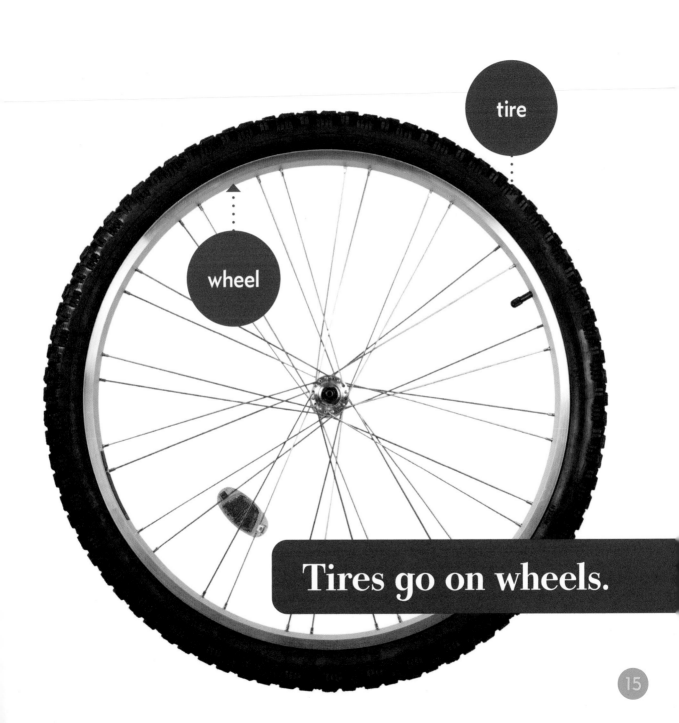

tire

wheel

Tires go on wheels.

Wheels are put on the frame.

Pedals are, too.

So is the chain!

handlebars

The handlebars
go on, too.

Don't forget
the seat!

We ride bikes.
Fun!

From Mining to Riding

How is metal made into bicycles that we can ride? Take a look!

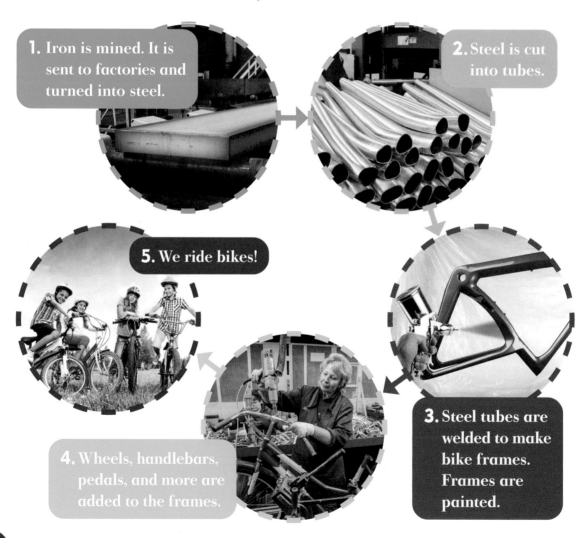

1. Iron is mined. It is sent to factories and turned into steel.

2. Steel is cut into tubes.

3. Steel tubes are welded to make bike frames. Frames are painted.

4. Wheels, handlebars, pedals, and more are added to the frames.

5. We ride bikes!

Picture Glossary

iron
A strong, hard metal.

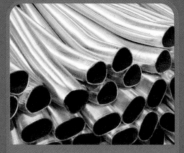

metal
A solid material, such as iron or steel, that is usually hard and shiny.

mined
Found in and taken out of the earth.

steel
A strong, hard metal that is made out of iron.

torch
A tool that produces a hot flame.

welds
Joins two pieces of metal by heating until they melt together.

Index

To Learn More

Finding more information is as easy as 1, 2, 3.

❶ Go to www.factsurfer.com

❷ Enter "frommetaltobicycle" into the search box.

❸ Choose your book to see a list of websites.